CONTENT

Introduction	02
What is an Axolotl?	04
Axolotl's Physical Features	12
Axolotl's Habitat	32
Axolotl's Lifestyle	38
Axolotl's Diet	55
Axolotl's Super Power	64
Axolotl Care	74
Interesting Trivia about Axolotls	94

INTRODUCTION

Hey there, young explorers! Are you ready to dive into the enchanting and mysterious world of one of the most extraordinary creatures on our planet? Grab your snorkels and flippers, because we're about to embark on an underwater adventure to discover the fantastic world of axolotls!

In this magical book, you'll uncover the secrets of these incredible animals that have captivated scientists and animal lovers alike. Did you know that axolotls are like real-life superheroes with amazing powers? They can regrow their limbs, heal without scars, and even regenerate their hearts! How cool is that?

Axolotls aren't just unique; they're also full of surprises. With their smiling faces and frilly gills, they take us on a journey to learn about the wonders of nature and the importance of taking care of our environment.

From the mystical waters of Mexico City's canals to the cozy tanks in our homes, axolotls have a story to tell, and it's nothing short of magical.

In these pages, you'll find fascinating facts, incredible insights, and fun tidbits about axolotls. You'll learn about their habitat, what they like to eat, and how they live their remarkable lives underwater. Plus, there are cool activities and quizzes to test your new-found knowledge about these amazing amphibians.

So, young adventurers, are you ready to meet these extraordinary creatures? Let's jump into the world of axolotls and uncover the secrets of their magical lives!

WHAT IS AN AXOLOTL?

Ancient Creatures: Axolotls have been around for millions of years. They are often considered living fossils because they have changed very little over time. This makes them like a window into the ancient past, showing us what creatures from long ago might have looked like.

Aztec Legends: The name 'axolotl' comes from the Aztec language, Nahuatl. It is often translated to mean "water monster," which is fitting given their unique appearance. According to Aztec mythology, the god Xolotl transformed into an axolotl to avoid being sacrificed and to hide from the other gods. This ties the axolotl to a story of transformation and mystery.

Only Found in Mexico: Axolotls are native only to Mexico, specifically to two high-altitude lakes near Mexico City: Lake Xochimilco and Lake Chalco. Lake Chalco no longer exists, but Lake Xochimilco still has axolotls, although they are now endangered in their natural habitat.

Surviving in a Changing World: Despite their ancient origins, axolotls have shown an incredible ability to survive and adapt to changing environments. They can even survive in water with low oxygen levels by breathing through their skin and lungs, a rare trait among amphibians.

A Creature of Many Forms: In the wild, axolotls are normally a dark color to blend into their murky lake environment. However, in captivity, they can be white with pink gills (known as leucistic), golden, or even albino, showing the variety of ways they can look.

Linked to the Ancient City of Tenochtitlan: The lakes where axolotls live were once close to the Aztec capital, Tenochtitlan. This ancient city was built on an island in the middle of a lake, much like the habitat of the axolotl.

A Delicacy Once Upon a Time: Historically, axolotls were considered a delicacy by the Aztecs. They were often consumed as a part of the local diet. This fact connects them deeply with the culture and history of the region.

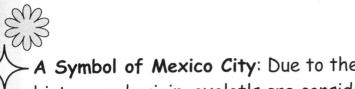

A Symbol of Mexico City: Due to their unique history and origin, axolotls are considered a cultural symbol of Mexico City and its natural history.

The Axolotl's Ancient Ancestors: Believe it or not, axolotls share a common ancestor with the tiger salamander. Millions of years ago, their evolutionary paths diverged, leading to the unique species we see today.

A Life in Permanent Childhood: One of the most astonishing things about axolotls is that they exhibit a trait called neoteny. This means they retain their juvenile features throughout their entire life. Unlike other amphibians that undergo metamorphosis to become land-dwelling creatures, axolotls remain aquatic and gilled all their lives.

Mysterious Lake Dwellers: The lakes where axolotls live are remnants of a vast water system that once covered the Valley of Mexico. These ancient lakes are thought to be over 12,000 years old, making the axolotl's habitat historically and geologically significant.

A Symbol of Mexico City: Due to their unique history and origin, axolotls are considered a cultural symbol of Mexico City and its natural history.

A Symbol of Adaptation and Survival: Axolotls are remarkable examples of adaptation. They've survived drastic changes in their environment over millennia, showing an incredible resilience and ability to thrive under different conditions.

Connected to the Sun and Fire: In Aztec mythology, the axolotl is not just linked to the water but also to the celestial. They were believed to be connected to the god Xolotl, who was associated with fire and lightning, as well as the setting sun.

A Creature of Night and Twilight: Axolotls are naturally nocturnal, preferring to hunt and be active during the night or at twilight. This behavior ties them to the mysterious and less-seen parts of the natural world.

A Creature of Night and Twilight: Axolotls are naturally nocturnal, preferring to hunt and be active during the night or at twilight. This behavior ties them to the mysterious and less-seen parts of the natural world.

The Changing Colors of Captivity: While wild axolotls are typically brown or black to camouflage in their natural environment, captive breeding has produced a variety of colors, including pink, golden, and even piebald patterns.

A Link to the Dinosaurs: Axolotls have been on Earth for a very long time, even coexisting with some dinosaurs. Their lineage dates back over 140 million years, which means they were around when some of the last dinosaurs roamed the Earth.

Survivors of Ancient Catastrophes: The axolotls' ancestors survived major events like the asteroid impact that caused the extinction of the dinosaurs. This resilience has allowed their species to continue until today.

Unique Breathing Abilities: Unlike many other amphibians, axolotls can breathe both through their gills and their skin. This unique adaptation allows them to absorb oxygen directly from the water, giving them a remarkable ability to live in environments with varying oxygen levels.

A Link to the Lost City of Tenochtitlan: The axolotl's natural habitat in the lakes around Mexico City is near the site of the ancient Aztec city of Tenochtitlan, which was built on an island in a lake. This proximity links them to one of the greatest pre-Columbian cities in the Americas.

From Salamanders to Axolotls: Axolotls evolved from a species of salamander. Over time, they adapted to their specific environment in the Mexican lakes, developing unique features different from their land-dwelling relatives.

The Master of Camouflage: In the wild, axolotls are masters of camouflage. Their natural muddy brown or black color helps them blend into the lakebed, making it hard for predators to spot them.

A Living Indicator of Environmental Health: Axolotls are considered an indicator species, meaning their health reflects the health of their environment. Scientists study axolotls to understand the impacts of environmental changes and pollution.

The Axolotl's Ancestral Home: Axolotls are exclusively native to the ancient water systems of Mexico City, but their ancestors roamed a much larger area. Over millions of years, their kind adapted specifically to the unique conditions of Lake Xochimilco and Lake Chalco.

A Species Shaped by Geography: The unique geographical features of the Valley of Mexico, including its high altitude and volcanic soil, have played a significant role in shaping the axolotl's habitat and, consequently, its evolution.

AXOLOTL'S PHYSICAL FEATURES

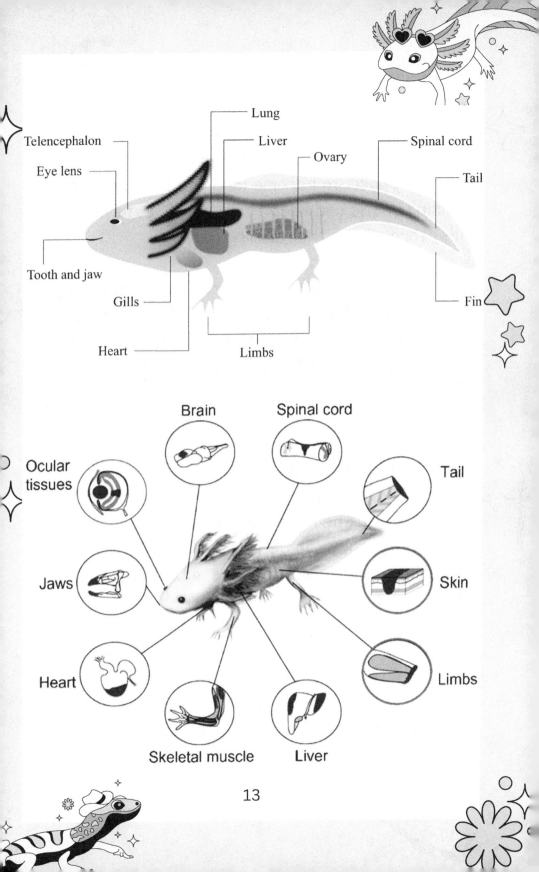

Perpetual Youth: The most extraordinary feature of axolotls is their perpetual larval state, known as neoteny. Unlike other amphibians that undergo metamorphosis to become land-dwellers, axolotls remain aquatic and keep their larval features (like gills) throughout their entire life.

External Gills: One of the most striking features of axolotls is their external gills. These feathery, branch-like structures protrude from behind their heads and are used for breathing underwater. They give axolotls a unique, otherworldly appearance.

Variety of Colors: In the wild, axolotls are typically dark green, brown, or black to help them camouflage in their natural environment. However, in captivity, they can be found in a range of colors, including white (leucistic), gold, albino (pink with red eyes), and even piebald.

Glowing in the Dark: Some captive axolotls have been genetically modified to glow under ultraviolet light. This is done for research purposes and demonstrates the axolotl's unique role in scientific studies.

Size and Growth: Axolotls can grow up to 12 inches (30 cm) long, but most average around 9 inches (23 cm). Their size can vary based on their environment and diet.

Lidless Eyes: Axolotls have distinctive eyes without eyelids. This is unusual among amphibians, many of which have movable eyelids.

Fin Along the Back: They have a dorsal fin that runs along their back and tail, which helps them swim. This fin is more prominent in the axolotl than in most other amphibians.

Regeneration Abilities: Not only can axolotls regenerate lost limbs, but they can also regrow parts of their brain, spine, and vital organs. This regeneration happens without scarring, making them a subject of intense scientific interest.

A Different Kind of Smile: Axolotls have a wide, almost smile-like mouth, which is part of their unique facial structure. Unlike many amphibians that have elongated or pointed faces, axolotls have a more rounded, flattened face.

Walking Underwater: While they are primarily swimmers, axolotls can also 'walk' along the bottom of their aquatic environment using their limbs. This is different from many amphibians, which are either purely aquatic or move to land after metamorphosis.

Lidless Eyes: Axolotls have distinctive eyes without eyelids. This is unusual among amphibians, many of which have movable eyelids.

Unique Skin Texture: Axolotls have a soft and smooth skin texture, unlike many amphibians that have rough or bumpy skin. This smooth skin helps them absorb oxygen and other necessary substances directly from the water.

No Need to Surface for Air: Unlike many aquatic amphibians that need to come up for air, axolotls can live their entire lives underwater thanks to their efficient gill-based breathing system.

Flexible Jaw Structure: Axolotls have a uniquely flexible jaw structure that allows them to open their mouths wide and consume a variety of prey, including small fish, worms, and insects.

Sensitive to Light: Due to their lack of eyelids and their evolution in murky lake environments, axolotls are particularly sensitive to light. In their natural habitat, they would spend most of their time in dimly lit waters.

A Tail for All Seasons: The axolotl's tail is not just for swimming; it also plays a role in their regenerative abilities. If they lose a part of their tail, they can regrow it, complete with its functional structure.

Balancing Act: The axolotl uses its tail and limbs to balance itself in water. This is important because, unlike many amphibians, axolotls do not have a strong terrestrial locomotive ability.

A Varied Diet: In the wild, axolotls are opportunistic feeders, consuming almost anything they can catch. This includes small fish, crustaceans, and even other smaller axolotls.

Temperature-Sensitive Creatures: Axolotls are very sensitive to temperature changes. They thrive in cool water and can become stressed in environments that are too warm, which is a contrast to many amphibians that require warmer temperatures to stay active.

Nocturnal Nature: Axolotls are primarily nocturnal, meaning they are most active during the night. This is a trait that helps them avoid predators and catch prey in their natural habitat.

Limited Vision, Enhanced Other Senses: While axolotls don't have the best vision, they compensate with a keen sense of smell and a lateral line system (similar to that in fish) that detects vibrations and movements in the water around them.

Tactile Tentacles: Axolotls have small, fleshy projections around their face, known as tentacles or feelers. These are not found in many amphibians and are used to sense their environment, helping them locate food.

Distinctive Teeth Structure: Unlike many amphibians that have tiny, almost invisible teeth, axolotls possess two types of teeth - tiny, sharp ones for gripping prey and flat ones for crushing it. This is unusual in the amphibian world.

Ability to Withstand Low Oxygen Levels: Axolotls can survive in waters with low oxygen levels, thanks to their efficient gill-based respiratory system and their ability to absorb oxygen through their skin.

Lack of Metamorphic Hormone: One reason axolotls don't undergo metamorphosis like other amphibians is due to their lack of thyroid-stimulating hormones, which are necessary for the process of metamorphosis.

Slow Movers, Efficient Hunters: Despite their relatively slow movement in water, axolotls are effective hunters. They rely on ambushing their prey rather than chasing it, a strategy that conserves energy.

Lateral Line System: Similar to fish, axolotls possess a lateral line system along their bodies. This system helps them detect minute changes in water pressure and movement, aiding in navigation and hunting in murky waters.

Floating Ribs: Axolotls have floating ribs, which are not attached to their sternum. This is different from many other amphibians, whose ribs are usually well-developed and attached.

Yawning Behavior: Axolotls exhibit a yawning behavior, which is unusual among amphibians. This behavior is thought to help them regulate pressure in their ears and is also used during feeding.

Selective Breeding for Unique Patterns: Through selective breeding, particularly in captivity, axolotls have been bred to have unique color patterns and variations. These include mottled, speckled, and even striped patterns, which are not commonly seen in wild axolotls.

Unusual Eye Development: Axolotls have a rare trait in their eye development. Unlike most amphibians that develop complex eyes after metamorphosis, axolotls maintain a larval form of eyes throughout their life, which limits their vision.

Specialized Feeding Adaptation: Axolotls have a highly specialized feeding adaptation that allows them to consume a variety of prey items. They have a wide gape and a muscular tongue, which aid in their suction feeding strategy.

Lack of a Middle Ear: Axolotls do not have a middle ear, which is common in other amphibians. This anatomical difference contributes to their unique hearing capabilities or lack thereof.

Reduced Bone Density: The bone density in axolotls is lower compared to many amphibians, particularly those that are fully terrestrial. This reduced density is linked to their entirely aquatic lifestyle.

Unique Fingertip Structures: Axolotls have unique structures at the tips of their fingers, which are different from other amphibians. These structures enhance their sense of touch, helping them to better navigate and hunt in their aquatic environment.

Differently Shaped Skull: The skull of an axolotl is flatter and wider than that of most amphibians, which typically have more elongated skulls. This skull shape supports their aquatic lifestyle and feeding habits.

Different Lung Development: Although axolotls have rudimentary lungs, they primarily rely on gills and skin for oxygen exchange. This is in contrast to most amphibians, which develop more functional lungs for breathing air after metamorphosis.

Variable Tooth Formation: Axolotls have a unique tooth formation. They continuously replace their teeth throughout their lives, which is not a common trait in most amphibian species.

Bloodless Cold Weather Survival: Unlike many amphibians, axolotls can survive in cold water conditions with minimal blood flow. This is a remarkable adaptation, as most amphibians require warmer temperatures.

Skin Sensitivity to Water Quality: The skin of an axolotl is extremely sensitive to the quality of water, more so than many other amphibians. This sensitivity requires very clean, well-maintained water conditions, especially in captivity.

Absence of a Tongue: Unlike many amphibians that catch prey with a long, sticky tongue, axolotls do not have this feature. Instead, they rely on their unique suction method to feed.

Unique Pattern of Muscle Development: The muscle development in axolotls is distinct, especially in their limbs. This is a result of their aquatic lifestyle and the need for swimming rather than walking or jumping like many terrestrial amphibians.

Differences in Skin Permeability: Axolotls have a different level of skin permeability compared to other amphibians. Their skin is specially adapted to their aquatic environment, allowing for efficient gas exchange and osmoregulation.

Limited Color Perception: Axolotls have a limited range of color perception. Their eyes are adapted for low-light conditions in murky waters, which means they don't perceive colors the same way many other amphibians do.

Distinctive Nervous System Adaptations: The nervous system of axolotls is adapted for their aquatic environment, showing differences in sensory and motor neuron arrangements compared to terrestrial amphibians.

Absence of Certain Defensive Mechanisms: Unlike some amphibians that have developed glands to secrete toxins or bright colors to warn predators, axolotls lack these defensive mechanisms. Their primary defense is their ability to camouflage and regenerative capabilities.

Tail Fin Structure: Axolotls have a distinct tail fin that extends beyond the tail tip, a feature not common in most amphibians. This tail fin aids in their swimming, allowing for more effective movement in water.

Specialized Gill Rakers: The gill rakers of axolotls are uniquely structured to filter out food particles from the water, a trait that is uncommon among other amphibians who generally do not rely on this feeding method.

Differing Larval Development: In most amphibians, the larval stage is a transition phase to adulthood. However, axolotls remain in this larval stage their entire life, a phenomenon known as paedomorphosis, which is quite rare in the animal kingdom.

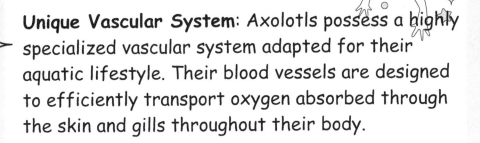

Unique Vascular System: Axolotls possess a highly specialized vascular system adapted for their aquatic lifestyle. Their blood vessels are designed to efficiently transport oxygen absorbed through the skin and gills throughout their body.

Exceptional Buoyancy Control: Axolotls have an extraordinary ability to control their buoyancy, allowing them to float motionless or sink to the bottom with minimal effort. This ability is different from most amphibians, which are either predominantly land-based or not as adept at controlling buoyancy.

Skin Microbiome: Axolotls have a unique microbiome on their skin that is vital for their health. This microbiome is different from those found on other amphibians and plays a critical role in protecting them from infections and diseases.

Differentiated Eye Anatomy: The eye anatomy of axolotls is quite different from other amphibians. Their retinas, for example, are adapted to their primarily underwater lifestyle, functioning better in low-light conditions.

Absence of Metamorphosis Triggering Hormones: Axolotls lack certain hormones that trigger metamorphosis in other amphibians. This hormonal difference is a key factor in why they remain in their aquatic, larval form throughout their life.

Adapted Lung Functionality: While axolotls do have lungs, they are rudimentary and not used for primary respiration. This is in contrast to many amphibians that rely on lungs more extensively after metamorphosis.

Unique Salamander Characteristics: While axolotls are classified as salamanders, their physical characteristics, such as the retention of gills and lack of eyelids, set them apart from most other salamander species.

Neural Crest Cells: Axolotls have a high concentration of neural crest cells, which play a significant role in their regeneration abilities. These cells, more abundant and versatile in axolotls than in most amphibians, can transform into different types of cells as needed for regeneration.

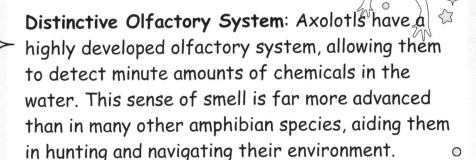

Distinctive Olfactory System: Axolotls have a highly developed olfactory system, allowing them to detect minute amounts of chemicals in the water. This sense of smell is far more advanced than in many other amphibian species, aiding them in hunting and navigating their environment.

Unusual Breeding Adaptations: Axolotls have a unique reproductive adaptation in that they can breed in their larval form. Most amphibians need to undergo metamorphosis and reach adult form before they can reproduce.

Differential Growth Rates: The growth rate of axolotls can vary significantly depending on environmental conditions, more so than in many other amphibians. This flexibility allows them to adapt to varying food availability and temperature conditions.

Robust Immune System: Axolotls have a remarkably robust immune system, particularly in their skin, which helps them resist infections in water - a trait that is not as pronounced in many terrestrial amphibians.

Unique Body Proportions: Compared to other amphibians, axolotls have a different body proportion, with a relatively larger head and shorter limbs. This body structure is adapted for their aquatic lifestyle.

Adaptation to Hypoxic Environments: Axolotls are exceptionally well-adapted to live in hypoxic (low oxygen) environments. They can survive in water conditions with much lower oxygen levels than what would be tolerable for most amphibian species.

Variation in Gill Morphology: The morphology of axolotls' gills varies greatly compared to other gilled amphibians. Their gills are larger, more branched, and external, which is a unique adaptation among amphibians.

Reduced Pigmentation Variability: In their natural habitat, axolotls exhibit less variability in pigmentation compared to other amphibians, typically displaying a dark coloration for camouflage. However, this has changed significantly in captive populations.

Particular Sensory Adaptations: Axolotls have sensory adaptations that are specifically suited for an aquatic environment, such as sensing pressure changes and detecting movements in water, which are more refined than in many amphibians that split their time between water and land.

Heartbeat Peculiarity: Axolotls have an unusually slow heartbeat for an amphibian, which can be as low as 60 beats per minute. This is in stark contrast to many smaller amphibians whose hearts beat much faster.

Particular Gill Morphology: Axolotls' gills are not only external but also have a unique structure with profuse branching, allowing for efficient oxygen absorption directly from water, a trait that is rare among amphibians.

Skin Texture Variability: In axolotls, the skin texture can vary significantly between individuals, from almost smooth to slightly rough. This variability is more pronounced in axolotls than in many other amphibian species.

Uncommon Eye Development: Axolotls develop their eyes differently from most amphibians. Their eyes grow slowly and reach full size only well into their adulthood, unlike many amphibians whose eyes develop rapidly after metamorphosis.

Distinctive Respiratory Adaptations: While most amphibians develop lungs and lose their gills as they mature, axolotls retain their gills throughout their life. Moreover, their lungs are rudimentary and mainly function as buoyancy aids rather than for respiration.

Specific Limb Structure: The limbs of an axolotl are uniquely structured, being shorter and more robust compared to those of other amphibians, which aids in their lifestyle as bottom-dwellers in water bodies.

Hypoxia Tolerance: Axolotls are extraordinarily tolerant of hypoxic conditions. They can survive in water with much lower oxygen levels than most amphibians, thanks to their ability to absorb oxygen through their skin and gills.

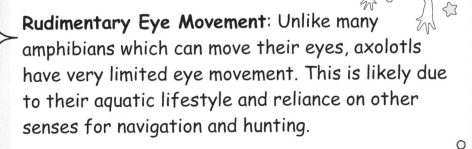

Rudimentary Eye Movement: Unlike many amphibians which can move their eyes, axolotls have very limited eye movement. This is likely due to their aquatic lifestyle and reliance on other senses for navigation and hunting.

Unusual Hemoglobin Properties: The hemoglobin in axolotl blood is specially adapted to carry oxygen efficiently, even in low-oxygen environments. This adaptation is different from most amphibians, whose hemoglobin is optimized for terrestrial environments.

Unique Skin Glands: Axolotls have specialized skin glands that secrete mucus, aiding in their underwater existence. This mucus plays a role in keeping their skin moist, protecting against infections, and facilitating smooth movement in water.

Peculiar Vertebrae Structure: Axolotls have a unique vertebrae structure compared to other amphibians. Their vertebrae are more simplified and fewer in number, which is an adaptation to their aquatic lifestyle.

A Unique Ecosystem in a Megacity: Axolotls are found in the ancient water system of Xochimilco, a network of canals and floating gardens, in the midst of Mexico City, one of the largest cities in the world. This juxtaposition of a unique natural habitat within a bustling urban area is rare.

The Remnants of a Vast Lake System: The Xochimilco area is what remains of a much larger lake system that once included the now-disappeared Lake Chalco. These lakes were part of the Valley of Mexico, an endorheic basin, which means they had no natural outlets.

Man-Made Islands for Agriculture: The 'floating gardens' or 'chinampas' in Xochimilco are an ancient agricultural technique of the Aztecs. These are small, rectangular areas built on the shallow lake bed, creating a patchwork of canals and land. This unique agricultural method has created a diverse and rich habitat for axolotls.

A Habitat Formed by Volcanic Activity: The Valley of Mexico, where Xochimilco is located, was shaped by volcanic activity. This has influenced the mineral content and the layout of the lake and canal systems, creating a unique environment for axolotls.

A Declining and Fragile Ecosystem: The natural habitat of axolotls is under significant threat due to urban expansion, pollution, and habitat destruction. The water quality of the canals has deteriorated, and invasive species have been introduced, posing a grave threat to the axolotl population.

Rich Biodiversity: Despite the threats, Xochimilco remains a hotspot of biodiversity. The canals and chinampas are home to numerous native and migratory bird species, fish, amphibians, and plants, creating a complex ecosystem in which axolotls play a crucial role.

Protected Area Status: The Xochimilco area is recognized as a World Heritage Site by UNESCO, highlighting its cultural and ecological importance. Efforts are ongoing to preserve this unique habitat, which is vital for the survival of axolotls in the wild.

A Cool and Stable Climate: The climate in Xochimilco is generally mild and stable, with temperatures that are ideal for axolotls. The water in the canals is cool throughout the year, which is necessary for the health and well-being of these amphibians.

The Challenge of Invasive Species: Invasive species such as tilapia and carp have been introduced into Xochimilco's canals. These fish compete with axolotls for food and space and can also prey on juvenile axolotls.

Cultural and Historical Significance: Beyond its ecological value, Xochimilco represents a significant cultural and historical landscape, reflecting ancient agricultural practices and sustaining a connection with Mexico's pre-Hispanic past.

Waterways of Historical Significance: The canals of Xochimilco are part of a water transport system that dates back to the pre-Hispanic era. These ancient waterways were crucial for transportation and commerce in the Aztec Empire.

A Closed Basin Ecosystem: The Valley of Mexico, where Xochimilco is located, is an endorheic basin, meaning it does not drain to the sea. This isolation has created a unique ecological niche, influencing the evolution of species like the axolotl.

Natural Filtering System: The chinampas, along with the natural vegetation in and around the canals, act as a biological filter. This system helps to maintain water quality, which is vital for the axolotls' survival.

Seasonal Variations in Habitat: The water levels in Xochimilco can vary with the seasons, influencing the availability of breeding and feeding areas for axolotls. They adapt to these changes by moving to different parts of the canals and adjusting their behavior.

A Refuge in an Urban Landscape: Amidst the urban sprawl of Mexico City, Xochimilco serves as a green refuge, harboring a rich diversity of flora and fauna. The contrast between the bustling city and this serene natural habitat is striking and underscores the importance of urban conservation efforts.

High Endemism: The isolation of the Valley of Mexico has resulted in a high level of endemism. Many species found in Xochimilco, including the axolotl, are unique to this region and cannot be found anywhere else in the world.

Role in Aztec Mythology and Culture: Xochimilco holds a significant place in Aztec mythology and history. The water and the life it supports, including the axolotl, have been revered and integrated into local cultural practices for centuries.

Unique Microclimate: The network of canals and floating gardens creates a microclimate that benefits the axolotls. This environment offers a stable temperature and an array of food sources, which are crucial for their survival in the wild.

High Endemism: The isolation of the Valley of Mexico has resulted in a high level of endemism. Many species found in Xochimilco, including the axolotl, are unique to this region and cannot be found anywhere else in the world.

AXOLOTL'S LIFESTYLE

Incredible Regeneration Abilities: Axolotls have an amazing ability to regenerate almost any part of their body, including limbs, tail, heart, and even parts of their brain. This means if they get injured, they can heal very quickly and completely, which is quite rare in the animal kingdom.

Expert Ambush Predators: In the wild, axolotls are stealthy hunters. They lie in wait, camouflaged in the murky waters, and when an unsuspecting prey comes near, they quickly snap it up using their wide mouths.

Life in Slow Motion: Unlike many animals, axolotls don't hurry. They move slowly and gracefully through the water, using their tail and tiny legs. This slow, gentle swimming makes them look like they are doing a water dance.

Night-Time Adventures: Axolotls are nocturnal, meaning they are most active at night. During the day, they like to hide under rocks or in the muddy bottom of their habitat, coming out to hunt and explore when it gets dark.

Incredible Regeneration Abilities: Axolotls have an amazing ability to regenerate almost any part of their body, including limbs, tail, heart, and even parts of their brain. This means if they get injured, they can heal very quickly and completely, which is quite rare in the animal kingdom.

Expert Ambush Predators: In the wild, axolotls are stealthy hunters. They lie in wait, camouflaged in the murky waters, and when an unsuspecting prey comes near, they quickly snap it up using their wide mouths.

Life in Slow Motion: Unlike many animals, axolotls don't hurry. They move slowly and gracefully through the water, using their tail and tiny legs. This slow, gentle swimming makes them look like they are doing a water dance.

Night-Time Adventures: Axolotls are nocturnal, meaning they are most active at night. During the day, they like to hide under rocks or in the muddy bottom of their habitat, coming out to hunt and explore when it gets dark.

Bottom Dwellers: In their natural habitat, axolotls spend most of their time at the bottom of the water body they live in. They like to stay close to the lake or canal bed, where it's safe and they can find plenty of food.

A Varied Diet: Axolotls aren't picky eaters. In the wild, they eat worms, insects, small fish, and even other small aquatic animals. They catch their food by sucking it into their mouths very quickly.

Sensing Their World: Even though axolotls don't have great eyesight, they are excellent at sensing movements and vibrations in the water. This helps them detect prey or predators nearby.

Breathing Underwater: Axolotls have gills that look like feathery plumes on the sides of their heads. These gills help them breathe underwater by extracting oxygen directly from the water.

Surviving in Murky Waters: Axolotls are well-adapted to living in water with low visibility. Their poor eyesight is compensated by their sensitivity to vibrations and movements in the water, helping them navigate and find food.

Silent Communication: Axolotls don't make any sounds. Instead, they communicate through body movements and changes in their coloration, a subtle but effective way to interact with each other, especially during mating season.

Winter Survival Strategy: In the colder months, axolotls slow down their metabolism. This means they need less food and move less, helping them survive when the temperature drops and food becomes scarce.

Egg-laying Habits: Female axolotls lay hundreds of eggs at a time. They carefully attach these eggs to plants or rocks in the water, where they remain until they hatch into tiny axolotl larvae.

A Life Without Sunbathing: Unlike many amphibians that bask in the sun to regulate their body temperature, axolotls spend their entire life underwater, away from direct sunlight. This is part of their unique adaptation as fully aquatic creatures.

The Young Are Self-Sufficient: Axolotl babies, or larvae, are independent from birth. They start hunting tiny organisms soon after hatching, not relying on their parents at all.

Change in Diet with Age: As axolotls grow, their diet changes. Young axolotls might start by eating small microorganisms, but as they get bigger, they can eat larger prey, like insects and small fish.

Masters of Stillness: Axolotls can remain incredibly still, almost like statues, when they are waiting for prey or trying to avoid being seen by predators. This stillness is a key part of their hunting strategy.

Limited Territorial Behavior: While axolotls are generally solitary, they don't exhibit strong territorial behavior like some animals. They might have a preferred spot, but they don't aggressively defend it from others.

Living in Cool Waters: Axolotls prefer cool water and are found in the chilly waters of their native Mexican lakes. They don't like it when the water gets too warm.

Adapting to Environmental Changes: Axolotls have shown remarkable adaptability to changes in their environment, such as fluctuations in water quality and temperature. This resilience is a testament to their ability to survive in varying conditions.

Remarkable Growth Cycle: Axolotls grow rapidly after hatching. From tiny larvae, they quickly grow into their full size, showcasing a fascinating and rapid growth cycle that is intriguing to observe.

Seasonal Feeding Patterns: Axolotls in the wild adjust their feeding habits based on the season. During warmer months, they might eat more due to higher metabolism, whereas in colder months, their feeding decreases as their metabolism slows down.

Use of Lateral Line System: Axolotls possess a lateral line system similar to fish, which allows them to sense changes in water pressure and movements. This system helps them detect prey and navigate their murky water environment effectively.

Selective Breeding Behavior: When it comes to breeding, axolotls are selective. They engage in complex mating rituals, and females choose which male's spermatophore to pick up, ensuring the best possible match for reproduction.

Specially Adapted Kidneys: Axolotls have kidneys that are well adapted to their aquatic environment. Their kidneys help them maintain the right balance of water and salts in their bodies, which is crucial for their survival in freshwater habitats.

Natural Detoxifiers: Interestingly, axolotls play a crucial role in their ecosystem by helping to keep the water clean. They feed on debris and waste material, acting as natural detoxifiers of their environment.

Survival Without Sunlight: Axolotls can survive in areas with very little sunlight. This is a unique adaptation, as many aquatic creatures rely on sunlight for various aspects of their life, including finding food and breeding.

Highly Efficient Oxygen Consumption: Axolotls have a remarkable ability to extract oxygen from water. Even in low-oxygen conditions, they can survive thanks to their efficient gill structure and ability to absorb oxygen through their skin.

Fascinating Foraging Technique: Axolotls use a fascinating foraging technique where they sift through the substrate and mud at the bottom of their habitat to find food, showcasing their adaptability in finding nutrition in a variety of ways.

Adaptation to Variable Water Conditions: Axolotls are adapted to live in various water conditions, from clear to muddy waters. Their ability to thrive in different water qualities is a testament to their resilience and adaptability in the wild.

A Life Without Transition: Unlike most amphibians that transition from water to land, axolotls spend their entire lives in water, never undergoing the transition to a terrestrial habitat. This constant aquatic lifestyle is unique among amphibians.

Efficient Oxygen Absorption Through Skin: Axolotls can absorb oxygen not only through their gills but also directly through their skin. This dual method of respiration is highly efficient and allows them to thrive in waters with varying oxygen levels.

Specialized Hunting Strategy for Larvae: Young axolotl larvae have a specialized hunting strategy. They primarily feed on small microorganisms and plankton using a unique, jerky swimming motion to catch their tiny prey.

Long Lifespan in the Wild: In the wild, axolotls can live longer than many other amphibian species, with lifespans reaching up to 10-15 years. This longevity is quite impressive for an amphibian.

Sensitivity to Environmental Changes: Axolotls are highly sensitive to changes in their environment, especially to water quality and temperature. This sensitivity makes them a good indicator species for the health of their ecosystem.

Surviving in Dimly Lit Waters: Axolotls have adapted to live in dimly lit waters, where visibility is low. This adaptation helps them ambush prey and avoid predators in their natural habitat.

Subtle Social Interactions: While axolotls are not highly social creatures, they do engage in subtle social interactions during breeding seasons and when sharing a common feeding area.

Growth Without Metamorphosis: As axolotls grow, they do not undergo metamorphosis but instead simply become larger versions of their larval form. This growth pattern is unique compared to other amphibians that change form as they mature.

Predation and Defense Mechanisms: In the wild, axolotls face threats from predators such as birds and larger fish. Their primary defense mechanisms include camouflage and their ability to quickly regenerate lost body parts.

Adaptation to Seasonal Food Availability: Axolotls in the wild adapt to seasonal variations in food availability. They can store energy and slow down their metabolism during times when food is scarce.

Surviving in Dimly Lit Waters: Axolotls have adapted to live in dimly lit waters, where visibility is low. This adaptation helps them ambush prey and avoid predators in their natural habitat.

Subtle Social Interactions: While axolotls are not highly social creatures, they do engage in subtle social interactions during breeding seasons and when sharing a common feeding area.

Growth Without Metamorphosis: As axolotls grow, they do not undergo metamorphosis but instead simply become larger versions of their larval form. This growth pattern is unique compared to other amphibians that change form as they mature.

Predation and Defense Mechanisms: In the wild, axolotls face threats from predators such as birds and larger fish. Their primary defense mechanisms include camouflage and their ability to quickly regenerate lost body parts.

Adaptation to Seasonal Food Availability: Axolotls in the wild adapt to seasonal variations in food availability. They can store energy and slow down their metabolism during times when food is scarce.

Responsive to Seasonal Daylight: Axolotls in the wild are attuned to the changing length of daylight across seasons. This sensitivity influences their breeding cycle and activity patterns.

Natural Predators: In their natural habitat, axolotls have to watch out for predators like herons, large fish, and even humans. They rely on their camouflage and quick reflexes for protection.

Indicative Growth Rings: Similar to trees, axolotls' bones develop growth rings. Scientists can study these rings to understand the age and growth conditions of an axolotl, which provides valuable insights into their lifestyle and environmental conditions.

Adaptability to Fluctuating Water Levels: Axolotls are adept at adapting to changing water levels in their natural habitat. During rainy seasons, they can explore expanded territories, while in dry seasons, they manage to survive in shrinking water bodies.

Selective Feeding Technique: Axolotls use a selective feeding technique, choosing prey based on size and ease of capture. They are known to be opportunistic feeders, eating what is available but preferring certain types of prey when they have a choice.

Limited Geographic Distribution: The wild axolotl population is confined to a very small geographic area, making their lifestyle and survival highly dependent on the specific conditions of their local environment.

Capacity to Withstand Polluted Waters: Remarkably, axolotls have shown a certain level of tolerance to polluted waters, a testament to their resilience. However, excessive pollution and habitat destruction remain significant threats.

Interaction with Other Aquatic Species: In their natural habitat, axolotls coexist with a variety of aquatic species. Their interactions with these species, from competition to cohabitation, play a role in the balance of their ecosystem.

Sensitivity to Light Pollution: Being nocturnal, axolotls are sensitive to light pollution. Excessive artificial lighting can disrupt their natural behaviors, such as feeding and breeding patterns.

Impact of Invasive Species on Diet: The introduction of invasive species in their habitat has impacted the axolotls' diet, forcing them to compete for food and adapt their feeding habits to the changing ecosystem.

Survival in Varied Substrates: Axolotls can adapt to a variety of bottom substrates in their natural habitat, from soft, muddy bottoms to rocky and leaf-littered surfaces. This adaptability allows them to thrive in diverse areas of their aquatic environment.

Shifting Breeding Sites: Depending on the conditions of their habitat, axolotls can change their preferred breeding sites. They are known to seek out the most suitable areas for laying eggs, often influenced by water temperature and quality.

Flexibility in Prey Size: Axolotls in the wild exhibit flexibility in the size of prey they consume. As they grow, they shift from feeding on small invertebrates to tackling larger prey, showcasing their adaptability as predators.

Vulnerability to Climatic Extremes: Despite their adaptability, axolotls are vulnerable to extreme climatic changes. Prolonged droughts or excessive rainfall can significantly impact their habitat, affecting their ability to find food and breed.

Navigation Skills in Murky Waters: Axolotls have developed excellent navigation skills to move through the often murky waters of their natural habitat. They use a combination of sensory inputs to orient themselves and locate food.

Occasional Cannibalism: In certain conditions, especially when food is scarce, axolotls may exhibit cannibalistic behavior. This is more common in densely populated environments where competition for resources is high.

Seasonal Activity Patterns: The activity level of axolotls can vary with the seasons. They tend to be more active during warmer periods and less so during colder months, aligning their behavior with environmental conditions.

Energy Conservation Strategy: Axolotls have a low-energy lifestyle compared to many other animals. They conserve energy by limiting their movements and only actively hunting when necessary, an efficient survival strategy in their habitat.

Impact of Water Currents: In their natural habitat, axolotls are accustomed to living in waters with minimal currents. They prefer calm, still waters where they can easily control their movements and hunt effectively.

Role in the Aquatic Food Chain: Axolotls play a significant role in their ecosystem's food chain. As both predators and prey, they help maintain the balance of their aquatic environment, impacting the population dynamics of other species.

AXOLOTL'S DIET

Carnivorous Appetite: Axolotls are carnivores, which means they eat other animals. In the wild, their diet consists primarily of meat.

Diverse Menu in the Wild: In their natural habitat, axolotls feast on a variety of prey, including small fish, worms, insect larvae, and crustaceans like shrimp. They are opportunistic feeders, eating whatever small animals they can catch.

Suction Feeding Technique: Axolotls have a unique way of eating called suction feeding. They open their mouths wide and suck in water along with their prey. It's like they have a built-in vacuum cleaner for catching food!

No Chewing Here: Axolotls don't chew their food. They swallow their prey whole, thanks to their wide mouths and flexible jaws.

Feeding on Small Prey: Young axolotls, or larvae, start by eating microscopic organisms in the water. As they grow, they shift to larger prey.

Adaptable Hunters: Depending on their environment and what's available, axolotls can adapt their diet. This flexibility helps them to survive in different conditions.

Cannibalistic Tendencies: In certain situations, especially in crowded environments, axolotls might exhibit cannibalistic behavior. Larger axolotls may eat smaller ones if there's not enough food to go around.

Captivity Diet: In captivity, axolotls are often fed a diet of bloodworms, brine shrimp, small strips of beef or liver, and specially prepared fish food pellets. This diet is designed to mimic their natural food as closely as possible.

Feeding Frequency: Unlike many animals, adult axolotls don't need to eat every day. They can be fed several times a week, which is enough to keep them healthy and happy.

Growth-Related Diet Change: As axolotls grow, their dietary needs change. Juveniles eat more frequently than adults, as they need more energy for growth and development.

Adaptable Hunters: Depending on their environment and what's available, axolotls can adapt their diet. This flexibility helps them to survive in different conditions.

Natural Foragers: In their natural habitat, axolotls spend a significant amount of time foraging for food. They use their keen sense of smell to locate potential meals in the murky waters of their environment.

Prey Detection Abilities: Despite their poor eyesight, axolotls are adept at detecting prey. They are sensitive to movements and vibrations in the water, which helps them hunt effectively even in low visibility.

Specialized Diet as Larvae: When axolotl eggs hatch, the larvae initially feed on the yolk sac from their egg for nourishment. As they grow, they quickly transition to consuming small organisms in the water.

Diet Impact on Coloration: The diet of axolotls can influence their coloration. In the wild, their natural prey contributes to their darker color, which aids in camouflage. In captivity, a different diet can lead to lighter coloration.

Role of Live Prey: Axolotls have a preference for live prey. The movement of live food stimulates their hunting instinct, making feeding more natural and engaging for them.

Occasional Plant Consumption: While primarily carnivorous, axolotls may occasionally consume plant material, particularly in captivity. However, this is not a major part of their diet.

Impact of Overfeeding: In captivity, it's important to avoid overfeeding axolotls, as they can become overweight. A balanced diet is crucial for their health and wellbeing.

Feeding Strategies Change with Age: As axolotls mature, their feeding strategies and preferences may change. Older axolotls might become more adept at catching certain types of prey.

Indicators of Health in Diet: The eating habits and appetite of axolotls can be indicators of their health. Changes in their eating behavior can signal issues that may need attention.

Dietary Changes with Seasons: In the wild, the diet of axolotls can change with the seasons. During certain times of the year, when specific prey is more abundant, their eating habits will adjust accordingly.

Nocturnal Feeding: Axolotls primarily hunt and feed at night. Their nocturnal habits are aligned with the behavior of many of their prey, which are also more active during this time.

Preference for Moving Prey: While axolotls can eat both live and dead prey, they have a natural inclination towards moving prey. This instinct is strong even in captivity, where they might be more stimulated to eat when their food is moving.

Ingestion of Sediments: Occasionally, axolotls might ingest small amounts of sediment while feeding on the bottom of their habitat. This incidental ingestion is natural given their bottom-dwelling hunting style.

Eating Strategy Post-Injury: If an axolotl loses a limb, its eating strategy might temporarily change while it regenerates the lost part. This incredible adaptation ensures their survival even when they're injured.

Use of Sensitive Whiskers: Around their head, axolotls have sensitive whisker-like structures that help them detect food in their surroundings. These whiskers enhance their ability to locate prey in murky waters.

Variable Eating Frequency: Young axolotls eat more frequently than adults due to their rapid growth needs. Adult axolotls can go longer between meals, which reflects their slower metabolism.

Sniffing Out Prey: Axolotls use their sense of smell to hunt. They can sniff out prey in the water, guiding them towards a potential meal even in complete darkness.

Size of Prey: The size of the prey axolotls can consume is limited by the width of their mouths. They typically target prey that can be swallowed whole or in large chunks.

Water Flow and Feeding: In their natural habitat, axolotls might use the water flow to their advantage when feeding, positioning themselves in places where prey is likely to pass by due to the current.

Detecting Prey with Sensory Cells: Axolotls have special sensory cells around their mouths that help them detect prey in the water. These cells can sense the tiny movements made by potential food sources, making axolotls efficient hunters.

Preference for Protein-Rich Foods: In the wild, axolotls have a preference for protein-rich foods. This high-protein diet is essential for their growth and regeneration abilities.

Efficient Energy Utilization: Axolotls are very efficient in utilizing the energy they get from their food. This efficiency is important for their survival, especially in environments where food might not be abundantly available.

Larvae Eating Habits: When axolotl eggs hatch, the larvae initially feed on the remnants of their egg yolk. After this, they quickly start hunting small organisms in the water, demonstrating their instinctual hunting abilities from a very young age.

Feeding as a Social Activity: In captivity, feeding time can become a social activity for axolotls. They often become more active and visible when they know food is coming, showing a level of interaction with their caregivers.

Adapting to Different Types of Prey: Axolotls can adapt their hunting strategy based on the type of prey available. This adaptability is a key survival trait in the varying conditions of their natural habitat.

Gulping Air for Buoyancy: Sometimes, axolotls gulp air from the surface of the water. While this is primarily for buoyancy control, it also plays a role in their feeding behavior, as it helps them position themselves better for capturing prey.

Survival Without Feeding: Adult axolotls have the remarkable ability to survive for extended periods without food if necessary. This adaptation is particularly useful in environments where food availability fluctuates.

Use of Tail in Hunting: Axolotls can use their tail as part of their hunting strategy, whipping it to help corner or stun small prey before eating them.

Interest in Varied Textures: In captivity, axolotls sometimes show an interest in the texture of their food. They may be more inclined to eat certain types of food based on how it feels in their mouth, a behavior that indicates their sensory engagement with feeding.

AXOLOTL'S SUPER POWER

Amazing Regeneration: Axolotls have the incredible ability to regenerate lost body parts. If they lose a limb, they can grow it back completely, with all the bones, muscles, and nerves in the right places. This regeneration process is so perfect that it's almost impossible to tell the new limb from the old one.

Regrowing Organs: Their power of regeneration doesn't stop at limbs. Axolotls can also regenerate parts of their vital organs, including their hearts and brains. This extraordinary ability is rare in the animal kingdom.

Healing Without Scarring: When axolotls heal from an injury, they don't form scar tissue like humans do. Their wounds heal perfectly, leaving no trace of the injury.

Cancer Resistance: Axolotls have a natural resistance to cancer. Scientists are studying them to understand why they don't develop cancer as often as other animals, including humans. This could lead to breakthroughs in cancer research.

Surviving Extreme Conditions: Axolotls can survive in conditions that would be challenging for other creatures. They can go for long periods without food, and their bodies can adapt to different levels of water quality and oxygen.

Master of Camouflage: In the wild, axolotls are great at camouflage. Their skin color and pattern help them blend into their natural environment, making them nearly invisible to predators.

Neoteny – Eternal Youth: Axolotls exhibit a trait called neoteny, meaning they retain their juvenile characteristics throughout their life. They stay in their larval form, with gills and a tail, and don't undergo metamorphosis like other amphibians.

Sensory Superpowers: Despite having poor eyesight, axolotls have an amazing ability to sense their environment using other means. They can detect tiny changes in water pressure and vibrations, helping them find food and navigate around.

Survival in Low Oxygen: Axolotls can survive in waters with low oxygen levels. They can breathe through their skin and gills, absorbing oxygen directly from the water.

Adaptability in Diet: Axolotls are adaptable eaters. They can adjust their diet based on what's available in their environment, which is crucial for their survival in the wild.

Cellular Transformation: Axolotls have cells called macrophages, which play a key role in their regeneration process. These cells can transform and aid in the healing process without causing inflammation or scarring, a capability that is highly unusual and valuable in medical research.

Incredible Neural Regeneration: Not only can axolotls regenerate their limbs and organs, but they can also repair their spinal cord and nerves. This means if their spinal cord is damaged, they have the ability to heal it and regain full functionality, which is almost unheard of in the animal kingdom.

Genetic Adaptability: Axolotls have a unique genome that is incredibly large and complex. This genetic makeup gives them the extraordinary ability to adapt and regenerate, making them a fascinating subject for genetic studies.

Resistance to Infections: During the regeneration process, axolotls are able to avoid infections in the wounded area. This natural resistance to infection in open wounds is a remarkable aspect of their immune system.

Hibernation-Like State: Axolotls can enter a state similar to hibernation if the conditions in their environment become too harsh. This state allows them to conserve energy and survive in less than ideal conditions.

Oxygen Efficiency: They have an exceptional ability to extract oxygen from water through their skin and gills, allowing them to thrive in environments where oxygen levels are low.

Rapid Wound Closure: When injured, axolotls can close their wounds rapidly, reducing the risk of infection and beginning the regeneration process almost immediately.

Extreme Temperature Tolerance: Axolotls can survive in a range of water temperatures, showing an impressive tolerance to environmental changes. This adaptability helps them endure conditions that would be challenging for many other aquatic animals.

Specialized Breathing Capabilities: Besides breathing through their gills and skin, axolotls can also gulp air from the water's surface and use their rudimentary lungs, showcasing a versatile respiratory system.

Unique Stress Response: Unlike many animals, axolotls show a unique response to stress. They can maintain regeneration and normal physiological functions even under stressful conditions, which is unusual in the animal world.

Extreme Genome Size: Axolotls have one of the largest genomes known in the animal kingdom. Their DNA is 10 times larger than that of humans, packed with genetic information that contributes to their incredible regenerative abilities.

Ability to Regenerate Multiple Times: An axolotl can regenerate the same body part multiple times. If it loses a limb several times, it can regrow it each time with the same efficiency and precision.

Tail Regeneration as Adults: Even as adults, axolotls can fully regenerate their tails, complete with the spinal cord, muscles, and skin. This ability remains effective throughout their lifespan.

Retaining Youthful Flexibility: Their neotenic state means axolotls retain the flexibility and growth potential of youth throughout their lives. This trait is key to their regeneration capabilities.

Morphological Plasticity: Axolotls demonstrate a remarkable morphological plasticity. This means they can adjust their physical form in response to environmental conditions, a rare trait in the animal kingdom.

Blood Vessel Regeneration: Beyond limbs and organs, axolotls can regenerate intricate networks of blood vessels in the regrown body parts, ensuring proper blood circulation in the new tissue.

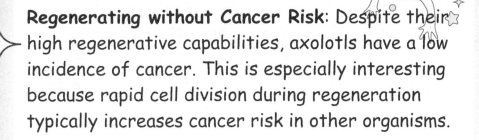

Regenerating without Cancer Risk: Despite their high regenerative capabilities, axolotls have a low incidence of cancer. This is especially interesting because rapid cell division during regeneration typically increases cancer risk in other organisms.

Partial Brain Regeneration: Axolotls are capable of regenerating parts of their brain, a feat that is virtually impossible for most other vertebrates, including humans.

Adaptable Metabolic Rate: Axolotls can adapt their metabolic rate according to the availability of food and environmental conditions, helping them survive in varying habitats.

Sensory Organ Regeneration: Not only can axolotls regenerate limbs and organs, but they can also regenerate certain sensory organs, maintaining their sensory capabilities throughout their lives.

Photoreceptor Regeneration: Axolotls can regenerate photoreceptors in their eyes, which means they can potentially restore lost vision – a capability that's highly unusual in the animal kingdom.

Reconfiguring Their Digestive System: During the regeneration of a lost limb, axolotls can reconfigure the digestive system to ensure the efficient allocation of energy and nutrients to the regrowth site.

No Aging in Regenerated Parts: Interestingly, the regenerated body parts of axolotls do not show signs of aging. The new limb or organ is as fresh and youthful as it was during the axolotl's early life stages.

Jaw Regeneration: Axolotls have the ability to regenerate parts of their jaw, including the bone and associated muscle tissues, maintaining their feeding efficiency throughout their life.

Muscle Regeneration Without Stem Cells: Unlike in many animals where stem cells are crucial for muscle regeneration, axolotls can regenerate muscle tissue without relying heavily on stem cells, a unique aspect of their regenerative process.

Coloration Regeneration: Axolotls can regenerate the coloration patterns on their skin along with the limb or tail, ensuring that the new part matches the rest of their body perfectly.

Nerve Regeneration Efficiency: Axolotls can regenerate their nerves more efficiently and faster than most other animals. This rapid nerve regeneration is critical in restoring full functionality to regenerated limbs.

Resetting Their Biological Clock: Each time an axolotl regenerates a body part, it's like resetting the biological clock for that part. The new tissue does not carry the wear and tear of the older cells, giving axolotls a unique advantage in longevity and health.

Adaptive Immune System During Regeneration: During the regeneration process, axolotls modify their immune response to prevent rejection of the regenerating cells, ensuring successful regrowth.

Unique Gene Expression for Regeneration: Axolotls express certain genes uniquely during regeneration, which are not active in other situations. These genes play a critical role in guiding the regeneration process effectively.

AXOLOTL CARE

Cool Water is Key: Axolotls need cool water to stay healthy. Their ideal water temperature is between 16°C and 18°C (60°F and 64°F). Warmer water can stress them out and make them prone to diseases.

Spacious Home: These creatures love space. A single axolotl needs at least a 10-gallon tank, but bigger is always better. More space means cleaner water and a happier axolotl.

Gentle Filtration: Axolotls don't like strong currents in their tank, as they naturally live in still or slow-moving waters. A gentle filtration system is best to keep their environment clean without stressing them.

They Like to Hide: In the wild, axolotls hide under rocks and plants. Replicating this in their tank with hiding spots like caves or plants (real or artificial) makes them feel safe and secure.

Special Diet: Axolotls eat a diet of worms, small fish, and special amphibian pellets in captivity. Feeding them the right amount is important – too much food can dirty their water, and too little can make them unhealthy.

No Gravel: Small gravel shouldn't be used in axolotl tanks. They might accidentally swallow gravel while feeding, which can lead to health problems. Fine sand or a bare-bottom tank is a safer choice.

Regular Water Checks: Keeping the water clean is crucial. This means regular water changes and checking the water's pH, ammonia, nitrite, and nitrate levels to ensure they stay within safe ranges.

Chill Company: Axolotls are generally solitary but can be kept with other axolotls if the tank is large enough. However, they should never be housed with fish or other aquatic animals, as they might hurt each other.

Hands-Off Approach: Axolotls can get stressed by too much handling. They are best enjoyed by watching them in their tank. Their delicate skin is also sensitive, so it's best to avoid touching them unless absolutely necessary.

Watching Their Health: It's important to keep an eye on an axolotl's behavior and appearance. Signs like refusal to eat, floating constantly, or lesions on their body can indicate health issues.

Lighting Needs: Axolotls don't require special lighting. In fact, they prefer dimly lit environments. Bright lights can stress them out, so it's best to keep their tank in a place with indirect, natural light or use low-intensity aquarium lights.

Tank Setup: Axolotls need a tank with a good amount of floor space because they are bottom-dwellers. A long tank is better than a tall one, ensuring they have plenty of room to move around at the bottom.

Water Hardness and pH: The water in an axolotl's tank should be slightly alkaline, with a pH between 7.4 and 7.6. The water hardness should also be monitored, maintaining it in a range that's comfortable for them.

Temperature Consistency: Keeping the water temperature consistent is crucial for axolotl health. Sudden changes in temperature can stress them and lead to health issues.

Safe Decorations: When decorating an axolotl tank, it's important to choose decorations that don't have sharp edges. Axolotls are delicate and can get injured by sharp or rough objects.

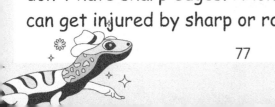

Avoiding Direct Contact: Axolotls have permeable skin, which means it's easy for them to absorb substances. This is why it's important to avoid touching them with hands that might have soap or lotion residues.

Observing Their Behavior: Regularly observing the axolotl's behavior can help in early detection of potential health issues. Healthy axolotls are usually active and have a good appetite.

Special Care for Regeneration: If an axolotl is regenerating a limb, it's important to keep the water extra clean to prevent infections and ensure a healthy regrowth process.

Use of Aquarium Salt: Sometimes, aquarium salt is used in axolotl tanks to help prevent fungal infections. However, this should be done cautiously and only under certain conditions, as axolotls are freshwater creatures.

Feeding Tools: To prevent overfeeding and keep the tank clean, feeding tongs or pipettes can be used. This also helps in feeding them specific amounts and avoiding waste.

Specialized Vet Care: If an axolotl gets sick, they need to see a vet who specializes in exotic pets or amphibians. Not all vets are familiar with axolotl care, so it's important to find the right expert.

Gentle Tank Cleaning: When cleaning their tank, it's important to be gentle. Harsh chemicals or soap should never be used as they can harm the axolotl. A simple rinse with water is usually sufficient for tank decorations.

Cycling the Tank Before Arrival: Before bringing an axolotl home, their tank needs to be cycled. This means setting it up with water and a filtration system and letting it run for several weeks to establish a balanced ecosystem.

Monitoring Their Growth: Keeping track of an axolotl's size can help ensure they are healthy and eating enough. A sudden change in size or growth rate can indicate a health issue.

Understanding Their Body Language: Axolotls can communicate stress or discomfort through their body language. For example, a curled tail tip or frayed gills can be signs of stress.

Moulting Process: Axolotls shed their skin as they grow. Unlike some reptiles, they usually eat the shed skin. This is completely normal and part of their natural behavior.

Avoiding Overcrowding: If keeping more than one axolotl in a tank, it's crucial to ensure they have enough space. Overcrowding can lead to stress and health problems.

Safe Substrate Choice: If choosing to use a substrate instead of a bare-bottom tank, fine sand is often recommended. It's less likely to cause impaction if accidentally ingested during feeding.

Regular Health Checks: Regularly checking the axolotl for signs of infection or injury, such as cuts or unusual spots on the skin, can help catch health issues early.

The Importance of Quarantine: If adding a new axolotl to a tank with an existing one, it's important to quarantine the new arrival first. This helps prevent the spread of any potential diseases.

Feeding Schedule for Young Axolotls: Baby axolotls, or larvae, need to be fed more frequently than adults – usually twice a day. This helps support their rapid growth and development.

Water Depth Matters: While axolotls are fully aquatic, they don't need very deep water. A depth that's about twice their length is sufficient, allowing them to comfortably swim and explore.

Keeping Their Water Oxygenated: It's important to keep the water in an axolotl's tank well-oxygenated. Using an air stone or a gentle filter can help circulate oxygen in the water.

Use of Plants in the Tank: Live plants are not just for decoration; they also contribute to the health of the axolotl's environment. Plants help oxygenate the water and can provide hiding places for axolotls.

Temperature Monitoring Is Crucial: Axolotls are sensitive to temperature changes. Using a reliable aquarium thermometer to regularly check the water temperature is essential to ensure their environment stays within the ideal range.

Handling With Care: If you need to handle an axolotl, it's important to do it very carefully. Using a soft mesh net or a plastic container is better than using hands, as their skin is very delicate.

Regular Tank Maintenance: Regular maintenance of the axolotl's tank is crucial. This includes partial water changes, checking the filter, and removing any uneaten food or waste to keep the environment clean and healthy.

Quiet and Calm Environment: Axolotls thrive in a peaceful environment. Keeping their tank in a quiet area of the house away from loud noises and heavy foot traffic can help reduce their stress.

Avoiding Direct Sunlight: The tank should be placed in an area where it won't be exposed to direct sunlight. Direct sun can rapidly change the water temperature and encourage the growth of algae.

Learning Their Eating Habits: Observing how your axolotl eats can provide insight into its health. A healthy axolotl is usually eager to eat, and any changes in appetite should be noted as it could indicate health issues.

Special Consideration for Their Gills: Axolotl's gills are very sensitive and crucial for their breathing. It's important to ensure that the water is not only clean but also free from strong currents that could damage these delicate structures.

Creating a Naturalistic Habitat: Setting up the tank to mimic their natural habitat can make axolotls feel more at home. This includes having a soft substrate, plants, and hiding spots that replicate the lakebed environment of their wild counterparts.

Regular Nail Trimming for Safety: If housing multiple axolotls together, it's important to regularly trim their nails. This helps prevent them from accidentally injuring each other.

Monitoring Tank Mates Closely: While axolotls can sometimes coexist with certain types of snails or shrimp, it's important to monitor these tank mates closely. Axolotls might try to eat smaller creatures, and some tank mates can be harmful to axolotls.

Variety in Diet for Optimal Health: Offering a variety of foods can ensure that axolotls get all the nutrients they need. A mix of earthworms, bloodworms, and specially formulated pellets can provide a well-rounded diet.

Avoiding Chlorinated Water: Tap water often contains chlorine, which is harmful to axolotls. Using a water conditioner to remove chlorine or letting tap water sit for 24-48 hours before use can make it safe for them.

Understanding Their Stress Signs: Learning to recognize signs of stress in axolotls is important. Signs like refusing food, floating excessively, or frantically swimming can indicate that something in their environment needs adjustment.

Engaging Observation Activity: While axolotls shouldn't be handled frequently, watching them can be a fun and educational activity. Observing their behavior can teach kids about aquatic life and the importance of caring for the environment.

Safe Handling of Food: When feeding axolotls, it's important to ensure that the food is safe. Live food should be sourced from reliable suppliers to prevent the risk of disease transmission.

Sensitivity to Metals: Axolotls are highly sensitive to metals. It's important to ensure that there are no metal objects in their tank, as metals like copper and zinc can dissolve in water and harm the axolotl.

Avoiding Overcrowding: If keeping more than one axolotl in the same tank, it's crucial to provide ample space to prevent stress and aggression. A general rule is to add an extra 10 gallons of water per additional axolotl.

Tank Lid is a Must: Axolotls can be surprisingly good at jumping, so having a secure lid on their tank is essential to prevent any adventurous escape attempts.

Regular Health Monitoring: Regularly monitoring the axolotl's skin and gill health is important. Any changes in color or texture can be early signs of health issues that need attention.

Controlled Feeding Environment: Creating a specific feeding area in the tank, like a shallow dish, can help keep the tank cleaner. Axolotls can learn to go to this area to eat, which can also make feeding time an interactive experience.

The Need for a Cycling Period: Before introducing an axolotl to a new tank, the tank needs to go through a cycling period to establish beneficial bacteria. This process can take several weeks and is crucial for the health of the axolotl.

Using Axolotl-Safe Cleaning Tools: When cleaning the tank, it's important to use tools that are designated only for the axolotl's tank to prevent contamination from household cleaners or other chemicals.

Temperature Monitoring Tools: Using a reliable aquarium thermometer to monitor water temperature daily is crucial. Sudden temperature changes can stress axolotls and lead to health problems.

Patience in Acclimation: When introducing an axolotl to a new tank, it's important to acclimate them slowly. Gradually adjusting them to the temperature and water chemistry of the new tank helps prevent shock.

Decor to Prevent Stress: Proper tank decoration is not just aesthetic; it helps reduce stress in axolotls. Plants and hiding places give them a sense of security and mimic their natural environment.

Mimicking Natural Daylight: Though axolotls don't need special lighting, mimicking natural daylight patterns can help maintain their natural circadian rhythms. This includes having periods of light and darkness that simulate day and night.

Understanding Their Mood Changes: Axolotls can change their behavior based on their mood and health. For example, a happy and healthy axolotl is usually curious and may come to the glass when someone approaches their tank.

Use of Sand Substrate: If choosing to use a substrate, fine sand is often recommended for axolotls. It's gentle on their delicate skin and reduces the risk of ingestion compared to gravel.

Bare-Bottom Tank for Easy Cleaning: Some axolotl owners prefer a bare-bottom tank for ease of cleaning. This can be especially helpful for maintaining water quality and monitoring the axolotl's health.

The Benefit of Snail Tank Mates: Certain types of snails can be beneficial in an axolotl's tank. They can help clean by eating algae and leftover food, but it's important to choose species that won't harm the axolotl.

Regular Water Testing: Testing the water regularly for ammonia, nitrites, nitrates, and pH levels is important. Keeping these levels in check is crucial for the axolotl's health.

Need for Gentle Handling: If it's necessary to handle an axolotl, it should be done gently and infrequently. Their skin is sensitive and handling can be stressful for them.

Avoiding Tap Water Toxins: Tap water often contains chlorine and chloramine, which are harmful to axolotls. Using a water conditioner to neutralize these chemicals is essential before adding water to their tank.

Soft Music Can Be Soothing: Some axolotl owners find that playing soft, calming music near the tank can have a soothing effect on their pets. However, loud noises should be avoided as they can be stressful.

Interactive Feeding: Feeding axolotls can be an interactive experience. They can learn to recognize the person who feeds them and may even follow their movements from inside the tank during feeding time.

Enrichment Activities: Like many animals, axolotls enjoy enrichment in their tanks. This can include gently rearranging their environment, introducing safe, axolotl-friendly toys, or changing up their feeding routine to keep them engaged and active.

Sensitivity to Sound Vibrations: While axolotls don't have great hearing, they are sensitive to vibrations. Keeping their tank in a low-traffic area where there's less noise and disturbance can help keep them calm.

Observing Their Breathing: Watching how an axolotl breathes can provide insights into their health. Rapid gill movement or frequent surfacing for air can indicate a problem with the water quality or their health.

Axolotls and Plants: Live plants not only oxygenate the water but also provide a more natural and enriching environment for axolotls. However, it's important to choose plants that can thrive in the same water conditions as axolotls.

Creative Tank Themes: Decorating an axolotl tank can be a fun and creative activity. Themes like a natural lakebed, fantasy settings, or prehistoric landscapes can make the tank an exciting focal point.

The Importance of Quarantine for New Additions: If introducing new plants, decorations, or tank mates, it's crucial to quarantine them first. This helps prevent the introduction of harmful bacteria or parasites.

Monitoring Growth: Keeping a growth chart or taking regular measurements can help track an axolotl's development and ensure they are growing at a healthy rate.

Tailored Water Flow: Creating a gentle water flow that mimics a slow-moving stream can provide a more natural and comfortable environment for axolotls, encouraging their natural swimming behavior.

Colorful Tank Mates: While axolotls should not be housed with fish, adding colorful, axolotl-safe decorations can make their environment visually stimulating for both the axolotl and its human observers.

Axolotls Can Recognize Their Owners: Over time, axolotls can recognize and react to the person who regularly feeds them and takes care of them, often becoming more active when that person is near the tank.

The Importance of Covering Intake Tubes: In a tank with a filter, it's important to cover intake tubes with a sponge or similar material. This prevents the axolotl's delicate gills from getting sucked into the tubes.

Axolotls Love Cool Toys: Safe, axolotl-friendly toys, like floating logs or tunnels, can provide enrichment and mimic hiding places they would find in the wild.

Gentle Tank Maintenance: When cleaning the tank, it's important to do it gently to avoid stressing the axolotl. Sudden movements or changes can be stressful for these sensitive creatures.

The Right Kind of Sand: If using sand as a substrate, it's important to use fine, soft sand. This reduces the risk of impaction if the axolotl accidentally ingests some while eating.

Monitoring for Signs of Stress: Signs of stress in axolotls include loss of appetite, listlessness, or scratching against objects. Recognizing these signs early can help address any issues promptly.

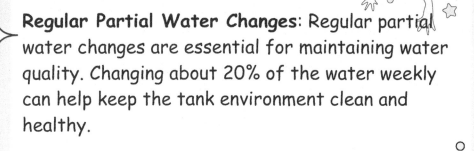

Regular Partial Water Changes: Regular partial water changes are essential for maintaining water quality. Changing about 20% of the water weekly can help keep the tank environment clean and healthy.

Avoiding Direct Handling: Axolotls are delicate and generally should not be handled unless necessary. Their skin is sensitive and can be easily damaged by human hands.

Learning Opportunity: Taking care of an axolotl provides a great learning opportunity about aquatic ecosystems, responsible pet ownership, and the importance of maintaining a stable and healthy environment.

Night Lights for Observation: Since axolotls are nocturnal, using a soft, dim night light near the tank can allow kids to observe their behavior during their active hours without disturbing them.

Axolotl First Aid Kit: Having a small first aid kit for the axolotl can be useful. It can include items for water testing, treatment for minor injuries, or fungal infections, under the guidance of a vet.

Trivia Question: What unique ability allows axolotls to regrow lost body parts?

    Answer: Axolotls have an incredible regenerative ability that allows them to regrow lost limbs, tails, and even parts of their heart and brain.

Trivia Question: Where are axolotls naturally found in the wild?

    Answer: Axolotls are native to only one place in the world – the lake complex of Xochimilco near Mexico City, Mexico.

Trivia Question: Why don't axolotls undergo metamorphosis like other amphibians?

    Answer: Axolotls exhibit a trait called neoteny, meaning they retain their juvenile features, like gills and aquatic lifestyle, throughout their entire life and don't undergo typical amphibian metamorphosis.

Trivia Question: What do axolotls primarily eat in the wild?

    Answer: In the wild, axolotls are carnivorous and primarily eat small fish, worms, insect larvae, and crustaceans.

Trivia Question: How do axolotls breathe underwater?

> **Answer**: Axolotls breathe underwater through their gills, which extract oxygen directly from the water. They can also absorb oxygen through their skin.

Trivia Question: What is a unique feature of axolotls' appearance compared to other amphibians?

> **Answer**: Unlike most amphibians, axolotls have external feathery gills on each side of their head, which are visible throughout their life.

Trivia Question: How can axolotls help humans in scientific research?

> **Answer**: Axolotls are used in scientific research due to their remarkable regeneration abilities. Studying them can provide insights into cell regeneration and healing, potentially benefiting medical research for humans.

Trivia Question: What is a common misconception about axolotls and their environment?

> **Answer**: A common misconception is that axolotls can live in any water condition. In reality, they need clean, cool, and well-oxygenated water to stay healthy.

Trivia Question: How do axolotls help maintain a healthy ecosystem in their habitat?

Answer: Axolotls help maintain a healthy ecosystem by being both predators and prey. They control populations of smaller creatures and provide food for larger animals, contributing to the ecological balance.

Trivia Question: What kind of animal is an axolotl, and how is it different from reptiles and fish?

Answer: An axolotl is an amphibian, specifically a type of salamander. Unlike reptiles, they have smooth skin and no scales, and unlike fish, they breathe through gills and skin, not just gills.

Trivia Question: Can axolotls change their color, and if so, how?

- **Answer**: Yes, axolotls can change their color, but it's usually influenced by their diet, age, and the environment. For instance, a change in diet can lead to a lighter or darker coloration.

Trivia Question: What does the name "axolotl" come from, and what does it mean?
- **Answer**: The name "axolotl" comes from the Nahuatl language, spoken by the Aztecs. It means "water monster."

Trivia Question: How do axolotls sense their environment, given their poor eyesight?
> **Answer**: Axolotls use a lateral line system, similar to fish, to sense vibrations and movements in the water, which helps them navigate and find food despite their poor eyesight.

Trivia Question: What unusual feature do axolotl eggs have compared to other amphibian eggs?
> **Answer**: Axolotl eggs have a unique sticky coating that allows them to adhere to surfaces underwater, like plants or rocks. This helps protect them from being washed away or eaten by predators.

Trivia Question: How long can axolotls live in captivity with proper care?
> **Answer**: With proper care, axolotls can live for up to 10-15 years in captivity, which is quite long for an amphibian.

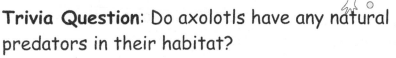

Trivia Question: Do axolotls have any natural predators in their habitat?
    Answer: Yes, in their natural habitat, axolotls have predators such as large fish and birds. However, their biggest threat is habitat loss and pollution caused by human activities.

Trivia Question: How do axolotls contribute to the cleanliness of their habitat?
    Answer: Axolotls help keep their habitat clean by feeding on debris and dead matter, acting as natural cleaners in their ecosystem.

Trivia Question: What is a unique characteristic of the axolotl's heart?
    Answer: A unique characteristic of the axolotl's heart is its ability to regenerate. Axolotls can repair their heart tissue, which is a rare ability among vertebrates.

Trivia Question: Why are axolotls often used in scientific and medical research?
    Answer: Axolotls are used in research because of their extraordinary regenerative abilities, which scientists hope can provide insights into human tissue regeneration and wound healing.

Trivia Question: Are axolotls social creatures?
- **Answer**: Axolotls are not particularly social creatures. They are generally solitary and can sometimes exhibit territorial behavior, especially during the breeding season.

Trivia Question: How do axolotls breathe if they spend their entire life underwater?
    Answer: Axolotls breathe primarily through their gills, which extract oxygen directly from the water. They can also absorb oxygen through their skin.

Trivia Question: What special feature do axolotl larvae have that helps them stick to surfaces?
    Answer: Axolotl larvae have suction cups on their heads when they're born, which help them stick to rocks and plants in the water.

Trivia Question: How can you tell the difference between a male and female axolotl?
    Answer: Male axolotls generally have longer, more slender bodies and a more swollen cloaca (the opening for excretion and reproduction) than females. Females are usually wider, especially when full of eggs.

Trivia Question: What happens to an axolotl's body temperature in different water temperatures?
    Answer: Axolotls are cold-blooded, or ectothermic, which means their body temperature changes with the temperature of the water. They depend on their environment to regulate their body temperature.

Trivia Question: Can axolotls live with other types of aquatic pets?
    Answer: Generally, it's not recommended to house axolotls with other types of aquatic pets, like fish or turtles, as they might harm each other or compete for food.

Trivia Question: What's unique about the way axolotls eat their food?
    Answer: Axolotls eat by suction feeding. They open their mouths wide to create a vacuum and suck in water along with their prey.

Trivia Question: Are all axolotls the same color?
    Answer: No, axolotls can have different colors. While wild axolotls are usually dark, captive axolotls can be black, white (leucistic), albino (pink with red eyes), golden, or even a combination of these colors.

Trivia Question: How do axolotls help keep their tank clean?
> **Answer**: While axolotls don't actively clean their tank, they eat small debris and food leftovers, which helps keep their environment tidy.

Trivia Question: Can axolotls hear sounds?
> **Answer**: Axolotls don't have external ears like humans, and their hearing is not well-developed. They primarily sense vibrations in the water rather than hearing sounds in the traditional sense.

Trivia Question: What do axolotls do most of the day in their natural habitat?
> **Answer**: In the wild, axolotls spend most of their time resting at the bottom of their aquatic habitat, coming out mainly to feed or during breeding season.

Trivia Question: What kind of environment do axolotls need in their tank to mimic their natural habitat?
- **Answer**: Axolotls prefer a tank setup that mimics a lakebed. This includes a soft substrate like fine sand, hiding places like caves or plants, and calm, cool water.

Trivia Question: How do axolotls communicate with each other?

> **Answer**: Axolotls mainly communicate through body language. They use movements and postures to signal things like territory, readiness to mate, or aggression.

Trivia Question: What is one of the biggest threats to axolotls in the wild?

> **Answer**: One of the biggest threats to wild axolotls is habitat destruction, primarily due to urbanization and pollution in and around Mexico City.

Trivia Question: Why are axolotls often called "Mexican walking fish"?

> **Answer**: Axolotls are sometimes mistakenly called "Mexican walking fish," even though they are not fish but amphibians. This nickname comes from their fish-like appearance and their habit of 'walking' along the bottom of their habitat.

Trivia Question: Can axolotls change color like some other amphibians or reptiles?
　Answer: Axolotls don't change color in response to their environment or mood like chameleons. However, their color can vary based on genetics, age, and diet.

Trivia Question: How do axolotls help scientists understand human health?
　Answer: Scientists study axolotls to learn about regeneration and how it could apply to human medicine. Their ability to regrow limbs and organs could help in developing treatments for injuries and diseases in humans.

Trivia Question: What do young axolotls eat compared to adult axolotls?
　Answer: Young axolotls, or larvae, eat small microorganisms and brine shrimp. As they grow, they start eating larger prey like worms and small pieces of meat.

Trivia Question: How can you tell if an axolotl is healthy?

    Answer: A healthy axolotl has clear eyes, a well-rounded body, responsive movements, and a good appetite. Their skin should be smooth without any cuts or sores.

Trivia Question: Why should axolotls not be kept in a tank with gravel?

    Answer: Gravel can be dangerous for axolotls because they might accidentally swallow it while eating, which can lead to digestive blockages.

Trivia Question: Do axolotls need companions in their tank?

    Answer: Axolotls are solitary by nature and do not require companions. They can live happily alone as long as their environmental and dietary needs are met.

Made in United States
Orlando, FL
08 May 2025